Contents ✔ KT-498-985

PREFACE

York Notes are designed to give you a broader perspective on works of literature studied at GCSE and equivalent levels. We have carried out extensive research into the needs of the modern literature student prior to publishing this new edition. Our research showed that no existing series fully met students' requirements. Rather than present a single authoritative approach, we have provided alternative viewpoints, empowering students to reach their own interpretations of the text. York Notes provide a close examination of the work and include biographical and historical background, summaries, glossaries, analyses of characters, themes, structure and language, cultural connections and literary terms.

If you look at the Contents page you will see the structure for the series. However, there's no need to read from the beginning to the end as you would with a novel, play, poem or short story. Use the Notes in the way that suits you. Our aim is to help you with your understanding of the work, not to dictate how you should learn.

York Notes are written by English teachers and examiners, with an expert knowledge of the subject. They show you how to succeed in coursework and examination assignments, guiding you through the text and offering practical advice. Questions and comments will extend, test and reinforce your knowledge. Attractive colour design and illustrations improve clarity and understanding, making these Notes easy to use and handy for quick reference.

York Notes are ideal for:

- Essay writing
- Exam preparation
- Class discussion

The author of these Notes is Dr Martin Stephen, High Master of The Manchester Grammar School and ex-Head of The Perse School, Cambridge. Educated at the Universities of Leeds and Sheffield, he is the author of fifteen books on literature and military history.

The text used in these notes is from the Mandarin paperback edition, published in 1995.

Health Warning: **This study guide will enhance your understanding, but should not replace the reading of the original text and/or study in class.**

PART ONE

INTRODUCTION

HOW TO STUDY A NOVEL

You have bought this book because you wanted to study a novel on your own. This may supplement classwork.

- You will need to read the novel several times. Start by reading it quickly for pleasure, then read it slowly and carefully. Further readings will generate new ideas and help you to memorise the details of the story.

- Make careful notes on themes, plot and characters of the novel. The plot will change some of the characters. Who changes?

- The novel may not present events chronologically. Does the novel you are reading begin at the beginning of the story or does it contain flashbacks and a muddled time sequence? Can you think why?

- How is the story told? Is it narrated by one of the characters or by an all-seeing ('omniscient') narrator?

- Does the same person tell the story all the way through? Or do we see the events through the minds and feelings of a number of different people?

- Which characters does the narrator like? Which characters do you like or dislike? Do your sympathies change during the course of the book? Why? When?

- Any piece of writing (including your notes and essays) is the result of thousands of choices. No book had to be written in just one way: the author could have chosen other words, other phrases, other characters, other events. How could the author of your novel have written the story differently? If events were recounted by a minor character how would this change the novel?

Studying on your own requires self-discipline and a carefully thought-out work plan in order to be effective. Good luck.

Early days John Ernst Steinbeck was born on 27 February 1902, in Salinas, California. The Salinas River is mentioned in the first line of *Of Mice and Men*, and the whole novel is centred on the landscape around Salinas. Steinbeck was the third of four children, of mixed German and Irish descent. His parents owned a considerable amount of land, and his mother was a schoolteacher who encouraged him to read widely. Whilst not particularly rich by American standards, his family were certainly not poor, and his upbringing was unremarkable. His early years followed a pattern familiar to many American middle-class children, in that his background was neither rich nor poor and his parents wanted him to follow a 'respectable' career.

Graduation He graduated from Salinas High School in 1919, having achieved minor sporting distinction and some success *Student jobs helped* writing for the school magazine. He went on to *shape Steinbeck the* Stanford University to study Marine Biology, but in *writer.* order to finance his studies had to take long periods away from university working to earn money. His jobs included clerk, shop assistant, waiter and labourer, as well as 'breaking army remounts for officers' gentle behinds'. This meant taking the semi-wild horses bought by the U.S. Army and rendering them fit to be ridden by officers. Throughout his life Steinbeck revealed a deep love of horses and dogs. Interestingly for anyone who reads *Of Mice and Men*, one of his jobs was as a ranch hand near King City. It was this experience he drew on most closely in writing the novel.

Taking a risk Steinbeck left University in 1925 without taking a degree and went to New York. His parents wanted him *Steinbeck challenged* to be a lawyer, a respectable career. He wanted to be a *his family and its* writer. For ten years he backed his decision, and seemed *values in order to be* set to be a total failure. To get to New York he had to *a creative writer.* work his passage as a seaman aboard a freighter. He was sacked as a reporter, left New York and took on a succession of temporary jobs. These included work as a caretaker, a mail coach driver and work in the local fish hatchery, Cannery Row near Monterey. There he met his first wife, Carol Henning, who had come to the fish hatchery as a tourist and met Steinbeck first of all as her guide. Steinbeck moved to San Francisco, where Carol had a job. They married in 1930.

Success

A key figure in Steinbeck's success was his father. He supported his son through the bleak years when he was trying to establish himself, giving him an allowance and letting Steinbeck and his wife live in the family's holiday home rent free. Outwardly there was little to justify his belief in his son. Steinbeck's first novel, *Cup of Gold*, was rejected several times before finding a publisher in 1929. It flopped.

His first novel failed financially.

McIntosh and Otis, literary agents.

Just as important for Steinbeck's success was the firm of McIntosh and Otis, who agreed to act as his literary agents in 1931. Steinbeck was loyal to his friends. In 1962, when he was awarded the Nobel Prize for Literature, he insisted that McIntosh and Otis take a percentage of the very considerable prize money, just as if the award had been a contract they had obtained for him.

It took until 1935 for Steinbeck to achieve his first real publishing success. In the ten years since he had left University without a degree, America had suffered a savage recession, hitting book sales as hard as anything else.

Steinbeck's second novel, *Pastures of Heaven* (1932) and his third, *To A God Unknown* (1933) were published by firms on the edge of bankruptcy. Amidst all this uncertainty, Steinbeck had to face the protracted and agonising illnesses of both his parents. His paralysed mother hung on for a year before finally dying in 1934.

Steinbeck's parents die.

But his father meant more to Steinbeck. He died in 1936, and for his last two or three years was a desperately unhappy and senile old man, physically incapable and mentally stagnant.

Commercial
success arrives.

Success came with *Tortilla Flat* (1935) and *Of Mice and Men* (1937). Both were a commercial success, both were eventually made into films. *Of Mice and Men* was turned into a play and won a Drama Critics award. It was also made the monthly selection of the Book of the Month Club, which guaranteed it huge sales. Steinbeck used some of the money to finance a trip he made with migrant workers in California.

This experience was to become the basis of what is probably still his best-known novel, *The Grapes of Wrath* (1939). It is one of the greatest novels to have come out of the United States this century. Before its publication, Steinbeck wrote to the publishers suggesting they only printed a few copies, as he did not think it would be successful.

Steinbeck the
man

Steinbeck was always a lonely man. Financial success removed some worries, but replaced them with a burden of fame that he found hard to handle. He was accused by right-wingers of being a revolutionary, a Communist and a Jewish sympathiser, none of which was true. Left-wingers damned him for not demanding a revolution.

Marriages and
divorces.

His marriage fell apart in 1940, when he met a professional singer called Gwendolyn Conger in Hollywood. He married her in 1942, produced two sons but was divorced again by 1948 on the grounds of incompatibility. He later said of his first marriage that it was the story of two people who hurt each other for eleven years, but he never lost touch completely with his first wife. It was, however, his third marriage, to

Elaine Scott in 1950, that brought him his greatest happiness in a relationship.

He moved in high circles in his later years, developing warm relationships with no less than three American presidents – Theodore Roosevelt, Lyndon B. Johnson and John F. Kennedy – but wrote only three books that are still widely read today, *Cannery Row* (1944), *East of Eden* (1952) and *The Winter of Our Discontent* (1961).

Nobel Prize for literature awarded, 1962. He was awarded the Nobel Prize for Literature in 1962, and died in 1968 of heart disease. He was buried in Salinas, California, a last return to the setting for *Of Mice and Men*.

How much should an author's personality influence judgements on his work? Steinbeck was a lonely, modest and restless man, never content and always searching for something more. He was a difficult man to live with, yet an easy one to love, something he shares with many great writers and artists. His love of the outdoors, of animals and of individual human beings shines through in *Of Mice and Men*. The joy of Steinbeck's birth and the sadness of his death were both centred on Salinas, California. The joy and the sadness which combine to make *Of Mice and Men* so remarkable a book revolve around that same place.

CONTEXT & SETTING

Examination boards increasingly insist, as does any good teacher, that you study a novel within its historical context. How much is *Of Mice and Men* affected by the times in which its author lived? How much is it a novel about those times?

Revolution and change In 1938, the year after *Of Mice and Men* was published, half of America's grain was harvested by mechanical combines. These machines required five men to do the work. Only a few years earlier, the same work had needed three hundred and fifty men for its completion.

Drastic changes were coming to the American economy and to American farming in the 1930s. In the 1880s grain was California's major product, and by 1900 some 125,000 'threshers' (almost always single men) were working the farms that stretched for 800 miles across the states of the Great Plains.

Migrant farm workers

George and Lennie are examples of the 'migrant' or 'itinerant' farm workers who fuelled and made possible this intensive farming economy. These men would travel great distances, either walking, using cheap bus services, hitch-hiking or travelling by train in the empty boxcars that were later used to ship out the grain they helped to farm. They would receive $2.50 or $3.00 a day, plus board (food) and a room. The food was basic, the room sometimes nothing more than a shared tent, but industrial action at the time of the First World War (1914–1918) had increased wages alongside an increase in the price of grain.

Social rankings divided farm workers.

The farm workers were almost a subculture, with their own social ranking. Thus before the days of mechanisation the mule driver was at the top of the social tree. A good mule driver could control a line of up to twenty mules single-handedly. Such a driver was regarded highly by the farm owner, who recognised how much work he could do and how much money he could save, but also respected by the farm workers themselves for his skill. Slim is just such a figure in *Of Mice and Men*. The reward for his skill is that he has permanent employment on the farm. Had he chosen to move, his skill could have commanded a high wage.

The American Dream

Many farm workers would share George and Lennie's dream of a 'smallholding' or small farm. Such an acquisition would allow men such as George to be their own master, and to make a decent if unspectacular living from the sweat of their own brow. Such a dream

y

is one part of the much larger phenomenon known as the American Dream.

The American Dream has it roots in the manner in which America was first populated. Its people came from almost every country and background, but were united by a belief that America would give them the opportunities denied them in their present country. For some, the lure was political or religious freedom from persecution. For very many others, America offered escape from grinding poverty or starvation. It was a new country and an undiscovered one. In Europe land had always been the key to financial independence and status. Only in America could the poor of Europe hope to settle virgin farmland. The frontier was expanding, gold fields were being discovered daily and waiting to be mined and mass immigration was presenting every possible opportunity for money, careers and reputations to be made.

An expanding frontier attracts immigrants.

At its simplest, the American Dream was the popular idea that America was a country that allowed men and women to make a clean start, to achieve prosperity and security. Like all dreams, the reality did not always match the dream. The destruction of the Native American population, the appalling horror of the American Civil War, the creation of ecologically disastrous urban and industrial slums, the corruption of many city managers were all growing pains of a new and great country. Yet the dream survived.

Death of a dream

That is, the American Dream survived until the late 1920s. By then there was no more frontier, no more virgin land to be claimed and America had built its own aristocracy on the basis of wealth and its own system of repression based on race.

Wall Street Crash, 1929.

The final blow was dealt by the Wall Street Crash, when the bottom fell out of stock market and share

12

prices. This marked the start of the Great Depression that was to sweep the whole world in the 1930s. Farming was as badly affected as any other area of the economy and decay there was speeded up by the fact that ignorance and over-farming had resulted in hundreds of thousands of acres of farmland drying up, losing their precious top soil and being turned into little more than desert. This was the creation of the famous 'dust bowl'. Poor crops meant that many of the farmers were unable to service the debts they had taken out in order to buy the land in the first place.

The 'dust bowl' forms.

Thus the way of life of men such as George, Lennie and Slim was coming to an end when *Of Mice and Men* was written, pushed by the twin forces of mechanisation and economic recession. President Roosevelt's New Deal policy was to go some way to boosting the economy, and the Second World War (1939–45) would finish the job. Neither could turn the clock back and reinvent the world lived in by George and Lennie.

Does George know that both Lennie and the dream have reached the end of their time?

Their dream of freedom and independence was probably doomed before they acquired it. Lennie makes George recite their dream to him at the end of the novel, not realising that George is preparing to shoot him before he is lynched by the pursuing mob. Lennie dies at George's hands, in an act of mercy. The dream they and many other migrant workers shared – 'We gonna get a little place' – is as doomed as Lennie.

Ordinary people

All the trends and events mentioned above had happened or were happening by the time *Of Mice and Men* was written. Is it therefore a novel about the end of the American Dream, about social change and about the exploitation of itinerant workers? Steinbeck knew about the changes. He cared about them. Yet the probable answer is that *Of Mice and Men* is a book about people, and a book which cares about people.

A book that cares about people.

Steinbeck does little probing of the reasons behind

social problems. He is concerned simply with looking at them as they are.

Do a simple test after reading *Of Mice and Men*. Would you have known about the Great Depression, the creation of the dust bowl and the increasing mechanisation of farming unless you had read a guide such as this? The answer is probably not. This knowledge helps you to understand the book. It does not explain it.

Salinas The countryside Steinbeck knew and loved is the background to the novel. The foreground is occupied by people who are human enough to have come from any area or region. This is not a novel about Salinas. It is a novel with Salinas in it.

Summaries

General summary

Pages 1–18: *Moving on*	One warm evening two men walk down from the highway to a pool by the Salinas River. George is small, dark and moves quickly, whilst it soon becomes apparent that Lennie, huge and blank-faced, is simple. They are off to take up work on a nearby ranch, but George tells Lennie not to say a word when they arrive; they have had to leave their previous job for some unspecified reason to do with Lennie. Lennie angers George by showing that he has kept a dead mouse to stroke its fur. George makes Lennie throw it away. Before they go to sleep, Lennie gets George to tell him a story he has obviously heard many times before, how when they have a little money they will run a small farm, with rabbits and other animals on it for Lennie to look after.
Pages 18–39: *Rising tensions*	They start work at the farm. The ranch owner questions Lennie but seems to accept that he is harmless. George and Lennie meet Curley, the violent, aggressive and argumentative son of the ranch owner. He has recently married a girl who is showing signs of wanting to be unfaithful to him. She comes into the bunk-house and flaunts herself. Lennie is attracted to her, and George becomes worried. Frightened that there will be trouble between Curley and Lennie, George arranges to meet Lennie by the pool where they spent the previous night, if there is any trouble. They meet Slim, the chief horse and mule driver, a man with natural authority.
Pages 40–69: *The dawn of* *hope*	Talking to Slim, George reveals that they were 'run out' of Weed, where they had previously been working, when Lennie was wrongly accused of trying to rape a

girl. Slim's dog has had a litter. Lennie is given a young puppy, and Carlson, a farm hand, makes Candy, an old man who cleans up round the farm, let his aged dog be shot, because it smells and is too old to be of any further use. Depressed by the loss of his dog, Candy hears George telling Lennie about their plans for a little farm, and offers to put up over half the money if they will let him come in with them. George finally begins to believe that his dream will become a reality. Curley breaks in, and starts a fight with Lennie. After taking a battering, Lennie crushes Curley's hand when George orders him to fight back. Slim makes Curley say that his hand was injured in an accident with a machine.

Pages 69–118: Death on the farm

One evening when nearly everyone has gone out to the local town, Lennie enters Crooks's hut. Crooks is a crippled and embittered negro who works on the farm in the stables. Lennie and Candy tell Crooks about their plan for a farm, but they are interrupted by Curley's wife, who threatens Crooks with a false rape charge when she is asked to leave the hut. Later Lennie kills the pup he has been given, not knowing his own strength. While he is trying to bury it in the straw on the floor of the barn Curley's wife comes in. They talk, and she asks him to stroke her hair. She panics when she feels Lennie's strength and by accident Lennie breaks her neck. When the body is found it is obvious that Lennie is the murderer. A hunt is started for him. George realises that Lennie could not bear life in prison, and cannot bear seeing him lynched by the farm hands who are hunting him. George goes to where he knows Lennie will be, and shoots him. Only Slim understands why he had to do this.

There are no chapter divisions in *Of Mice and Men*. The book falls naturally into four separate sections, as detailed below.

PAGES 1–18 (MOVING ON)

This section covers pages 1–18, and ends with the sentence, 'The sycamore leaves whispered in a little night breeze.'

George and Lennie are introduced.

The book opens with a description of the country around the Salinas River, south of Soledad in California. Two men come down to a pool by the river from the highway. George is small and dark, Lennie huge and ponderous. Lennie drinks from the stagnant water of the pool and is told off for so doing by George. The two men are heading for work on a nearby ranch, but have been dropped short of their destination by a bus driver. It is obvious that Lennie is simple, and George makes him get rid of a dead mouse that he has been petting in his pocket.

George coaches Lennie, 'the crazy bastard'

Before the two men settle down to share three cans of beans for supper, George gives Lennie strict instructions not to say anything when they meet the boss of the ranch the next day, because if Lennie does speak the boss will realise 'what a crazy bastard' (p. 6) he is. George has decided to spend the night in the open. Lennie asks why they do not go straight to the ranch, where there will be food. George says it is because they are starting hard work tomorrow, and he wants to savour the freedom of sleeping out in the open. George sends Lennie off to get wood for a cooking fire. When he returns George spots that Lennie has retrieved the dead mouse. George takes it from Lennie, who does not want to give it up, and throws it as far away as he can, because it is no longer 'fresh' (p. 10).

Accusations in Weed forced George and Lennie to flee.

It emerges that in Weed, where they were previously working, Lennie stroked the material of a girl's dress. She was frightened and tried to break away. Lennie clung on and the girl accused Lennie of trying to rape her. George and Lennie had to hide in an irrigation ditch and flee the town. George gets angry with Lennie, firstly because looking after Lennie limits George so much in what he can do, and secondly because Lennie keeps on getting both of them into trouble. Lennie is very hurt, and offers to leave and go and live in a cave. Lennie also plays cleverly on George's guilt at having thrown away the mouse.

The dream is explained.

George relents, and as the sun sets he tells Lennie a story they have obviously been through very many times, so many that Lennie knows part of it off by heart. It is their dream, about how they are going to buy a few acres of land, raise their own animals and live an independent and happy existence. They will have rabbits on the farm, and Lennie will be allowed to tend these and all the other animals. Comforted by the repetition of their dream, they go to sleep.

Y

COMMENT

Use of colour

Look how many different colours (green, yellow, gold and white) and how many different animals (lizard, racoon, rabbit, dog and deer) are mentioned in the first, short paragraph. Steinbeck has a very powerful descriptive style. Look how detailed it is: it is the 'lower leaf junctures' (p. 1) that are green, and he even notes that the deer's tracks are 'split-wedge' (p. 1). Also note Steinbeck's use of direct speech. The two characters give us information about what they think and about their personalities by how they talk.

Animal metaphors

Lennie is described by comparing him to a variety of animals. We call such descriptions metaphors (see Literary Terms). What effect does this have on us? Some readers think it is a mistake to describe him as a 'terrier' (p. 9), as these dogs are small creatures and Lennie is so huge. Others argue that the relationship between George and Lennie is like that between a master and his dog.

Warm colours and soft sounds combine to create an air of peace and contentment. Yet right at the end of the book the water-snake that was swimming peacefully in the river at the start of the novel is plucked out and eaten by a heron. Steinbeck uses this image (see Literary Terms) to warn us that nature combines peace and violence, with sudden swings from one to the other. We must therefore expect something similar for the humans who live so closely in this world.

Suspense

Steinbeck withholds information from us to build up suspense and interest. We know that something went wrong in Weed; we have to wait to find out what it was.

Innocence and danger

Lennie loves to pet mice, but kills them when he does so. This is a clear warning about how dangerous Lennie can be. Does his innocence and his unawareness of the threat he poses make him more or less menacing?

MOVING ON

GLOSSARY   **jungle-up** to make camp or spend the night somewhere

Murray and Ready's an agency set up as a result of President Roosevelt's New Deal which directed agricultural and other workers to where there was employment

work cards the evidence that Lennie and George had been sent by Murray and Ready's

thrashin' machines machines which separate out the grain in a corn crop (see Revolution and change in Context & Setting)

bindle a bundle of clothes and cooking utensils made portable by wrapping blankets round the outside

cat house brothel

work up a stake earn and save up money

blow their stake waste the money people have saved

poundin' their tail working very hard, to breaking point

blowin' our jack wasting our money

A ... *Identify the speaker.*

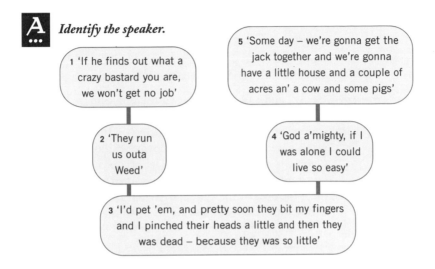

1 'If he finds out what a crazy bastard you are, we won't get no job'

5 'Some day – we're gonna get the jack together and we're gonna have a little house and a couple of acres an' a cow and some pigs'

2 'They run us outa Weed'

4 'God a'mighty, if I was alone I could live so easy'

3 'I'd pet 'em, and pretty soon they bit my fingers and I pinched their heads a little and then they was dead – because they was so little'

Identify the person(s) 'to whom' this comment refers.

6 'Wonder he isn't too damn good to stop in Soledad at all'

7 'Lady, huh? Don't even remember who that lady was'

Check your answers on page 67.

B ... *Consider these issues.*

a The inevitability of the novel's end helps build up suspense and makes *Of Mice and Men* more tragic.

b How much is the novel written in the style of a play, in terms of:
- dialogue (see Literary Terms)
- six play-like 'scenes'
- its use of light
- a small number of characters
- big events, such as the arrival of the mules, occuring 'off stage'
- few direct author statements

Does this explain why the novel was successfully turned into a play?

c Why does George want to spend the night out in the open, instead of going to the farm?

PAGES 18–39 (RISING TENSIONS)

This section runs from pages 18–39, starting with, 'The bunk-house was a long, rectangular building …' and ending at, 'the grizzled head sank to the floor again'.

A quick tour of the bunk-house with Candy.

George and Lennie are shown the bunk-house by Candy, the old man who cleans out the farm buildings. Candy lost his hand whilst working on the farm, and was allowed to stay on in this lowly position as cleaner. George is worried in case the last occupier of the bunk left it infested with lice, but is reassured by Candy. They meet the boss of the ranch, quite a reasonable man whose only real weakness seems to be that when he is in a bad mood he loses his temper with the negro who runs the farm stable. He is suspicious of George and Lennie, but is eventually satisfied that they will do good work for him.

Curley, the boss's son, comes into the bunk-house looking for his father. Curley is an ex-lightweight boxer who is always picking fights with people, and who seems to have a particular grudge against people bigger than himself. He is very concerned about his wife, who he married a fortnight ago, because she is giving all the

*Curley argues
with Lennie.*

men on the ranch 'the eye', suggesting she wants to sleep with them. Curley almost immediately picks an argument with Lennie. George is convinced that there will be trouble between Curley and Lennie. He warns Lennie to meet back where they camped the previous night if there is any trouble.

Curley's wife comes into the bunk-house. She uses the excuse that she is looking for Curley, but does not seem to want to leave. Lennie is fascinated by her and George tries to warn him off.

*We meet Slim, the
'jerkline skinner'.*

George and Lennie then meet Slim, the 'jerkline skinner' (see Glossary). Slim is a man of great dignity and natural authority. They also meet Carlson, a ranch hand. Carlson reveals that Slim's dog has had a litter of puppies. He suggests that Slim might give one of the pups to Candy, whose old dog is infirm and stinks out the bunk-house. Lennie becomes highly excited at the possibility of being given one of the puppies himself. Curley comes into the bunk-house again, looking for his wife and there is an immediate increase in tension.

C OMMENT

*Charac-
terisation*

This section introduces us to the main characters at the ranch. Again, characterisation is undertaken through dialogue (see Literary Terms). Each character has their own different way of speaking – look at sentence length, use of slang, repetition and accents.

Characterisation is also achieved through other methods. Candy's dog is old and physically infirm, with nothing to look forward to except death. Is the owner, Candy, being characterised at the same time as his dog, by association?

Curley is shown as thoroughly dangerous and foul. He claims to keep a glove on one hand full of Vaseline (a lubricating petroleum jelly), to improve his sexual performance. This is another example of a physical image (see Literary Terms) which describes the mentality of the character.

One of Steinbeck's special skills is unusual and therefore vivid descriptive language, as when he talks of Curley's wife's hair as being, 'in little rolled clusters, like sausages' (p. 32).

How is George's physical and mental cleanliness emphasised in this section?

The description of George putting his few possessions on to the shelves round his bunk is somehow pathetic, revealing how little such men have that is their own, and how rootless their life is. Slim is intrigued by George and Lennie going around together. He points out how rare this is, and how lonely and isolated most migrant ranch workers are.

GLOSSARY   **burlap ticking** coarse cloth, also known as hessian, covering the bedding on the bunk

roaches cockroaches

pants rabbits lice, fleas

swamper a cleaner, someone in a menial or degrading job

grey-backs lice

tick mattress cover

stable buck the negro ('buck') who looks after the stables

skinner driver of a horse or mule team

bum steer false or misleading information

bucker loader

rassel load

canned sacked or dismissed

jerkline skinner the jerkline is the single rein that runs to the lead animal in a team of mules or horses. A jerkline skinner is someone who can control the whole team by use of this one rein

eatin' raw eggs a suggestion that Curley is having to take extravagant measures in order to keep up his virility and satisfy his wife

two bits twenty-five cents in American money; an insignificant amount

in the poke saved up

wheeler's butt the flank of the lead animal

y

A Identify the speaker.

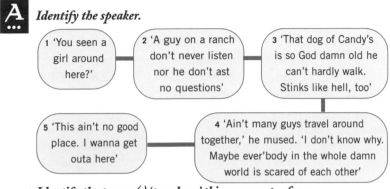

1 'You seen a girl around here?'

2 'A guy on a ranch don't never listen nor he don't ast no questions'

3 'That dog of Candy's is so God damn old he can't hardly walk. Stinks like hell, too'

5 'This ain't no good place. I wanna get outa here'

4 'Ain't many guys travel around together,' he mused. 'I don't know why. Maybe ever'body in the whole damn world is scared of each other'

Identify the person(s) 'to whom' this comment refers.

6 'Well, he's a pretty nice fella. Gets pretty mad sometimes, but he's pretty nice'

8 There was a gravity in his manner and a quiet so profound that all talk stopped when he spoke. His authority was so great that his word was taken on any subject, be it politics or love

7 'He hates big guys. He's alla time picking scraps with big guys'

Check your answers on page 67.

B Consider these issues.

a How Steinbeck illustrates his concern for the crippled and the elderly.

b The idea that a novel can change society. Though Steinbeck does not preach revolution, he does show clearly how much power 'the boss' has. This power extends to Curley being protected from the consequences of some of his actions, because even though the boss is a 'pretty nice fella' no one will tell him the truth about his son or his son's new wife.

c Almost immediately on arrival George has to defend Lennie, firstly against the boss and then against Curley, and finally against himself. This reveals how secure George's relationship is with Lennie. Think about what it reveals about the world outside their relationship.

PAGES 40–69 (THE DAWN OF HOPE)

Running from pages 40–69, this section starts at, 'Although there was evening brightness showing through the windows of the bunk-house …' and finishes with, 'Well, get the hell out and wash your face.'

Lennie gets a puppy.

George and Slim talk.

It is evening in the bunk-house. Slim has given a puppy to Lennie, and he and George talk. George feels able to tell Slim why he looks after Lennie. They were brought up in the same town, and when Lennie's Aunt Clara died Lennie came out to work with George. George says that he just got used to working with Lennie, and things developed from there. George also tells Slim how they came to be chased out of Weed. Lennie stroked the material of a girl's dress, and hung on in panic when she began to scream. She accused Lennie – wrongly – of rape and they had to hide all day up to their necks in water in an irrigation ditch to escape capture.

Lennie tries to take his puppy to bed with him, but is stopped by George. Carlson cannot stand the smell of Candy's old dog and asks Slim to give Candy one of the pups so that the old dog can be shot. The decision is postponed briefly when a young ranch hand shows Slim a letter in one of the western magazines that the hands love to read, written by a hand who used to work

Candy's dog is shot.

at the ranch. An unwilling Candy allows Carlson to take away his dog and shoot it. He is deeply upset.

George and Whit, another ranch hand, talk about Susy's, a local brothel where the men go on Saturday nights, and discuss Curley's wife. Curley bursts in and, seeing Slim is not there, rushes out thinking Slim is with his wife.

George and Lennie discuss the dream.

Lennie comes in and he and George start dreaming out loud about the little farm they are going to buy. Candy asks if such a farm actually exists. George says that he

knows one owned by old people who might be willing
to sell for $600 or so. Candy confesses he has $350
saved up and asks if he can come in with them. For the
first time George really begins to believe that his dream
might become a reality. All he needs to do is work for
another month or two and not spend anything and they
will have the stake to buy the farm.

Curley attacks
Lennie.

The mood is shattered when Slim and Curley burst in,
Slim furious at being falsely accused by Curley over his
wife. Curley turns on Lennie, and attacks him viciously.
At first Lennie does nothing, but responds when
ordered to fight back by George and crushes Curley's
hand. There is hardly a bone in the hand that is not
broken, but before Curley goes off to hospital Slim
makes him promise to say that his hand was damaged
in a machine, thus diverting any blame from Lennie.

COMMENT

Dreams and
reality

Curley's intervention is carefully timed to shatter the
dream-vision that George, Lennie and Candy have
built up. It is the heron killing the water-snake again, a
reminder that dreams can exist for only a short while in
the real world. It is also a reminder that the world can
be violent, cruel and unforgiving.

THE DAWN OF HOPE

George admits that early on being with Lennie made George feel superior, and made him order Lennie to do stupid things so that he could show off the authority he had over Lennie and laugh at him. He now realises how bad this was. So why does he stay with Lennie? The answer is given partly by George, whose comments reveal the utter loneliness of the life of an itinerant farm hand.

What 'dream' might George and Lennie have if alive now? The ranch hands outwardly scorn the Wild West magazines that they buy, but secretly they lap up the romanticised, glamorous view they give of cowboys and, by association, of ranch hands. The magazines show the workers how they would like to be. This is another dream, similar to that of George and Lennie. It will never be real, but it is necessary for surviving in the real world.

The importance of lighting Note the importance that light plays in Steinbeck's description. Much of the atmosphere in the discussion between Slim and George is created by the pool of light that the shaded lamp throws in the bunk-house.

Note also how delicately Steinbeck handles the discussion about the brothel. It could easily become coarse and obscene. In Steinbeck's hands it becomes natural, a normal part of a man's life. This is not to justify the use of prostitutes, but it shows how Steinbeck refuses to impose a politically correct agenda on to his writing. Steinbeck is concerned to reveal what the men think and feel, not to prove a point about what they ought to think.

GLOSSARY   **horse-shoe game** throwing horseshoes at an upright post with the object of encircling it
fifty and found a wage of fifty dollars a week, plus board and lodging
euchre card game for two people
yellow jackets wasps, stinging insects
flop sexual intercourse

kewpie doll lamp a lamp with a doll of a young child or an infant as its base

clean free from sexually transmitted diseases

getting burned getting infected with sexually transmitted diseases

bow-legged a symptom of syphilis, a sexually transmitted disease

Golden Gloves a boxing tournament

hoosegow prison

San Quentin a famous prison

alfalfa lucerne, a crop grown for feeding cattle

candy-wagon a trap or buggy, or carriage used for transporting people and not for farm work

A *Identify the speaker.*

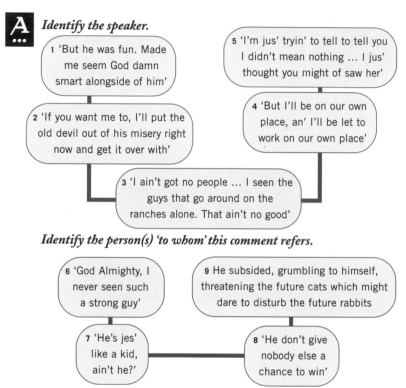

1 'But he was fun. Made me seem God damn smart alongside of him'

5 'I'm jus' tryin' to tell to tell you I didn't mean nothing ... I jus' thought you might of saw her'

2 'If you want me to, I'll put the old devil out of his misery right now and get it over with'

4 'But I'll be on our own place, an' I'll be let to work on our own place'

3 'I ain't got no people ... I seen the guys that go around on the ranches alone. That ain't no good'

Identify the person(s) 'to whom' this comment refers.

6 'God Almighty, I never seen such a strong guy'

9 He subsided, grumbling to himself, threatening the future cats which might dare to disturb the future rabbits

7 'He's jes' like a kid, ain't he?'

8 'He don't give nobody else a chance to win'

Check your answers on page 67.

B *Consider these issues.*

a The human need for companionship. The book presents a bleak vision of loneliness and powerlessness.

b The nature of hopes and aspirations. George seems to believe in his dream, but perhaps he is just repeating it to comfort Lennie and himself. Curley's violence and its destructive consequences may also suggest that all hopes are ultimately doomed.

c The motives of Curley's wife. She can be viewed as similar to Eve in the Bible, and once George and Lennie encounter her they lose their dream of paradise. Steinbeck thought this version a little harsh, and saw her rather as a confused, sexually inexperienced woman who was to be pitied more than anything else.

d Sexism in the novel. Think about how Steinbeck portrays women.

PAGES 69–113 (DEATH ON THE FARM)

This section runs from pages 69–113, starting at, 'Crooks, the negro stable buck, had his bunk in the harness-room' and ending at, 'Now what the hell ya suppose is eatin' them two guys?'

George has gone into town with the other ranch hands, leaving Lennie. Lennie walks into Crooks's room, and disarms his initial hostility with his simplicity. Lennie reveals the plan to buy a farm, but the cynical Crooks teases Lennie about what will happen if George does not come back from town. Crooks is frightened by Lennie's response and reveals how lonely he is as a crippled negro on a farm of white men.

Crooks teases Lennie.

Candy enters the room, this being the first time he has done so in all his years on the ranch. He talks about the farm he is going to move to with George and Lennie. Crooks pours scorn on the idea, as he has seen hundreds of men with a similar dream, but seems to be being won round when he realises how much of the money is actually there in the bank. He asks if he can come to work on the farm when it is bought, but he is interrupted by the appearance of Curley's wife.

The dreams of Curley's wife.

She reveals her loneliness, and her pathetic dreams of being an actress, as well as asking how Curley damaged his hand. Candy tries to stand up to her with his new-found confidence in owning a part of his own small farm, but she crushes him. She also crushes Crooks, threatening him with a rape charge, a crime for which a negro would be hung without trial. Crooks withdraws his request to join the farm, his treatment from Curley's wife acting as a forcible reminder of the truths of his life.

Lennie kills his puppy.

Lennie is in the barn stroking his puppy which he has killed by accident. Curley's wife, bored and restless, enters and insists on sitting beside him. Lennie tries to stop her, remembering George's advice to have nothing to do with her, but she insists and talks about her life. She is convinced that she could have joined a travelling show as a fifteen year old and become an actress. Another man she met at a dance promised her a part in the pictures, but he never wrote as promised to her. Convinced that her mother stole the letter, she married Curley out of spite and to get away from home.

The killing of Curley's wife.

She gets Lennie to admit that he likes stroking soft things and makes him stroke her hair. He strokes too hard and she cries out, frightening Lennie and making him cling on to her. When she will not stop screaming Lennie shakes her and by accident breaks her neck. He creeps away to the hiding place agreed with George.

Candy discovers the body and brings George, guessing the murderer must be Lennie. George and Candy realise this is the end of their dream. George slips back to the bunk-house, so as not to be implicated in the murder. Candy tells the others, and Slim guesses it must be Lennie who has broken her neck. They all set off to find Lennie, armed with shotguns.

Lennie waits for George in the clearing by the pool. He sees a vision of his Aunt Clara, which reprimands him.

The giant rabbit comes to Lennie as a vision.

It is then replaced by a vision of a giant rabbit which tells Lennie that George will now leave him, after what he has done. Lennie is crying out for George when he appears. George talks quietly and apparently calmly to Lennie, and repeats the old story in a wooden voice. The sound of the hunters draws near.

George kills Lennie.

George tells Lennie to look away from him, across the river, to where he will almost be able to see the farm that they will buy. He shoots the unsuspecting Lennie in the back of the head with Carlson's Luger pistol. Curley, Carlson, Slim and the others arrive, drawn by the shot. Only Slim understands what is going through George's mind. The two leave the others and go off down the highway for a drink.

COMMENT

The lull before the storm.

The section with Crooks, Candy and Lennie in Crooks's room is almost a rest period before the final climax. Many authors step down the tension a little before a major climax, almost as if to rest the reader before a very demanding section.

The tragedy of Curley's wife.

We are made to feel a lot of sympathy for the crippled negro, but also feel some sympathy for Curley's wife. She is a pathetic figure, with her own unrealisable dream, married to a man she hates and with nothing to do except stare that marriage in the face. In her own way she is as much of a victim as Lennie.

Terse style

As the climax approaches Steinbeck includes fewer descriptive passages and adopts a shorter, more terse style.

There is a tremendous irony (see Literary Terms) in the fact that George takes Carlson's pistol in case he has to kill Lennie as an act of mercy. Unfortunately, Lennie is assumed to have stolen the pistol. The result is that the pursuers adopt a shoot to kill policy, ensuring that Lennie will die whatever happens.

DEATH ON THE FARM

Curley's cruelty is revealed when he advises everyone to shoot for Lennie's stomach first of all, to double him up.

Are the three lines, 'As happens sometimes, a moment settled and hovered … much, much more than a moment' (pp. 97–8) too 'poetic', too rich in comparison with the rather objective, detached style Steinbeck adopts elsewhere? Or do these words capture a terrible moment in its entirety, standing out because they are so unusual?

Lennie's visions.

Some critics have condemned the two visions Lennie sees as being unrealistic and totally beyond the ability of a limited mind to generate.

Is the ending realistic?

Lennie is not allowed to escape again or just to be captured like any other murderer. Is the ending too artificial, too obviously designed for effect rather than being true to life? Why cannot George and Candy still set up their small farm? Or is the last section, with George and Lennie together for the last time, immensely powerful and moving?

Note how the novel ends on a marvellous image (see Literary Terms) of the sun blazing on the Gabilan Mountains.

GLOSSARY

hame part of the collar of a horse or mule
booby hatch lunatic asylum
made a ringer threw the horseshoes on to the peg
bull's-eye glasses spectacles with lenses that bulge outwards
gingham dyed cotton or linen, with a simple check pattern

TEST YOURSELF (Pages 69–113)

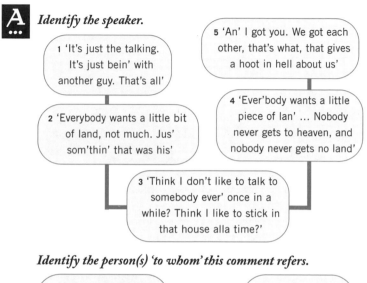

 A *Identify the speaker.*

5 'An' I got you. We got each other, that's what, that gives a hoot in hell about us'

1 'It's just the talking. It's just bein' with another guy. That's all'

2 'Everybody wants a little bit of land, not much. Jus' som'thin' that was his'

4 'Ever'body wants a little piece of lan' ... Nobody never gets to heaven, and nobody never gets no land'

3 'Think I don't like to talk to somebody ever' once in a while? Think I like to stick in that house alla time?'

Identify the person(s) 'to whom' this comment refers.

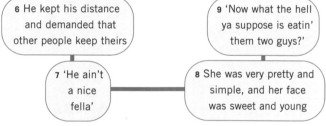

6 He kept his distance and demanded that other people keep theirs

9 'Now what the hell ya suppose is eatin' them two guys?'

7 'He ain't a nice fella'

8 She was very pretty and simple, and her face was sweet and young

Check your answers on page 67.

B *Consider these issues.*

a As the book progresses its ending becomes inevitable.

b The dream achieves its most powerful expression in this section, when it almost has the cynical Crooks believing in it. But the dream is also revealed in all its weakness when it collapses so easily.

c Think about the paradox (see Literary Terms) of a dream that people need to survive but which can never actually happen.

d The portrayal of Crooks is both a study of loneliness and a condemnation of racism.

PART THREE

COMMENTARY

THEMES

FATE AND DESTINY

Robert Burns

Sometimes a novel will hint at its theme (see Literary Terms) through its title. The title of *Of Mice and Men* appears to be taken from the poem 'To a Mouse' by the Scottish poet Robert Burns (1759–96),

> The best laid schemes o' mice and men
> Gang aft agley
> And leave us nought but grief and pain
> For promised joy!

Best laid schemes go wrong.

It is not difficult to see the link with Steinbeck's novel. 'Gang aft agley' means 'often go wrong'. George and Lennie's best laid scheme for a small farm does go wrong, and leaves grief and pain where there should have been joy. Burns's poem also suggests that grief and pain, instead of joy, are the lot of all creatures in nature, not just humanity. At the heart of the poem is the feeling that we are free to make our plans and lay our schemes, but far less free or likely to achieve them. Steinbeck never suggests that the likelihood of grief and pain should be a reason to stop humans laying their plans. We need to have these plans or dreams in order to survive, for all that they might hurt us.

The mention of mice by Burns also suggests something small and puny pitted against something overwhelmingly strong in the shape of Fate or Destiny. George and Lennie, and their dream, are similarly destined to be thwarted and shattered by inevitable forces over which they have no control.

This is perhaps the overriding theme of the novel – that humanity is small and fragile in comparison with the forces that control our lives, and that joy is something to be snatched while possible, but not something that most humans ever achieve for long.

There is no real thematic link between the mice in the title and the mice that Lennie likes to stroke. Lennie's mice are used rather as a motif (see Literary Terms) that echoes his vulnerability throughout the novel.

DREAMS AND REALITY

One of Steinbeck's themes (see Literary Terms) in *Of Mice and Men* is the dreams that people have. George and Lennie's dream is of a very small farm, a patch of land which they own themselves. It is a dream of working for themselves, of being independent, and it is a dream sufficiently powerful to draw in Candy and, temporarily, even the cynical Crooks. We know also it is a dream shared by many thousands of itinerant ranch hands.

Yet this is not the only dream in the novel. Curley's wife has a pathetic dream of being a movie star. The ranch hands dream of being the cowboy heroes they read about in the pulp magazines.

The American Dream   Some commentators have tied the dreams in the novel to a particular American Dream. For many years America welcomed the persecuted, the poor and the disadvantaged of the world, and if offered them the frontier. The line of civilisation steadily extended forward into virgin land until it reached the west coast. For those years the frontier was a line beyond which people were conditioned to believe that civilisation did not exist. Beyond it there was land for the taking, and a free and independent way of living where a man was answerable only to himself. People's old lives became history and new lives and new people could be created. Or so the story went. In truth the frontier was probably never like that, but the dream was necessary for people's survival and the belief that it might be true offered *The end of the* huge comfort to those who would never find out for *frontier.* themselves. By 1900 there was no more frontier, and many commentators believe that a new sense of pessimism crept into American culture. The hope of freedom, the hope of being an individual rather than a cog in a wheel, is certainly there in *Of Mice and Men*. So is the pessimism, because the dream is shattered, and shown to be unrealisable in the real world.

It would be wrong to confine the dream only to American society. Steinbeck is using an American example to illustrate a general truth, the need people have to dream of a life that is better and which will combine freedom and personal fulfilment. The peasant farmer dreaming of the extra pig, the businessman dreaming of what the next promotion will bring, the young child fixing his eyes on the soccer or the rock star are all dreaming. Like George and Lennie, the dream will come true for only a very few, and those few are likely to find that achieving a dream rarely avoids stark reality.

PESSIMISM OR OPTIMISM?

Is *Of Mice and Men* a pessimistic book? Its ending is unhappy, yet much in it is optimistic. George's care for Lennie, Lennie's adoration of George and the natural dignity of Slim are all positive, good things. Nor is Lennie's death wholly pessimistic. Lennie dies at the hand of the one man he trusts, painlessly, happy, free, in the open and still believing in his dream, as perhaps he might have died on the farm had they ever bought it.

An act of kindness. Lennie's death is an act of kindness, not of vengeance. To claim what happens as a good or a bad thing might be as senseless as to complain about the water-snake that is killed by the heron at the end of the book. Both are parts of life and nature, so inevitable that human comment on them is almost superfluous.

A balanced book. One of the key features of the book is balance, between the good and the bad, the happy and the unhappy. The dream is never realised, yet much good has been generated by the dreaming. Steinbeck never lectures you. He shows a vision of life that is neither black nor white. It has the simplicity of black, and the simplicity of white. He asks that you see life as it is, black and white side by side, rarely merging into grey.

PROTEST

Another frequently asked question is the extent to which *Of Mice and Men* is a political novel, or a novel of protest. The ranch hands get their fifty dollars a month and keep, seem to eat well and have a reasonable boss. To that extent the novel is not political. Nor does it concern itself with how the country is governed. If it protests it does so against three social and political evils: racial discrimination, the treatment of old age and the plight of the farm worker who never reaps what he sows.

Racial prejudice Crooks illustrates racial prejudice. He is intelligent, reads books and, like any other human being, he needs warmth and companionship. He is denied these not through any fault of his own but because he is a negro. Yet if there is a theme (see Literary Terms) of racial prejudice here it is almost a sub-division of a wider theme, that of loneliness.

Ageism Candy is older than Crooks, and is a man who has outlived his usefulness. He is waiting to be cast on the scrapheap with no more ceremony than a worn out domestic machine. Here again the larger and wider theme is one of loneliness, emphasised by Candy's relationship with his dog and his feelings when the dog is shot.

Both Candy and Crooks are workers who will never see the benefits of their labour.

LONELINESS

Loneliness is a major theme (see Literary Terms) in *Of Mice and Men*. George and Lennie stave it off by their relationship. It embitters Candy and Crooks. It kills Curley's wife. Steinbeck sees loneliness as a part of the human condition, something we are born with and something we either fight or succumb to all our lives:

> 'Guys like us, that work on ranches, are the loneliest guys in the world' .... Lennie broke in. '*But not us! Because .... because I got you to look after me, and you got me to look after you, and that's why*' (pp. 14–15)

Steinbeck offers no answers. As with many of the statements in the novel, Steinbeck offers no answers to loneliness, merely a graphic and moving portrayal of the problem. It confirms the impression of him as a writer who observes and brings things to life through the printed word, not someone writing with a grand game plan for how to change things. Indeed, some of the sadness and emotional power of the novel comes from our realisation that things cannot and will not change. .

MYTH AND NOBILITY

Arthurian legend Steinbeck was fascinated by the 'Arthurian legend', essentially the story of England's King Arthur and his Knights of the Round Table. A real Arthur seems to have existed in the 6th century, but bore no relationship to the romantic figure of the later Middle Ages. The story that was created then, most notably by Sir Thomas Malory (d. 1471) in *Le Morte D'Arthur*, has exerted huge power ever since. Two modern manifestations of it are in the Disney film *The Sword in the Stone*, based on the book by T.H. White, and the film *Excalibur*. Arthur's story has become a myth (see Literary Terms) – a story which seems to encapsulate a number of issues crucial to the experience of humanity, so crucial that the story is guaranteed to be recycled and recycled as each new generation arrives. Such myths have great power. That power is often attractive to an author. By their very survival myths have great strength and power over an audience or readership, and so by basing a story round a myth an author can tap into some of that myth's strength and appeal.

The power of myths.

All of this might seem a long way off from George and Lennie. After all, there are few knights in armour or round tables in the book, and the characters are essentially lower class, not the nobility of the Arthurian legend. Yet the Arthurian legend has the Knight and the Squire team at its heart, leadership and service, which is the relationship between George and Lennie. The legend is also based on two pivotal points – the search or 'quest' for the Holy Grail (the cup that Christ drank from at the last supper before his crucifixion), and the betrayal of Arthur by his wife (Guinevere) and best friend (Sir Lancelot). George and Lennie's search for their piece of land is a quest for something that will bring peace to them, their farm bearing some comparison to the Holy Grail. There is also betrayal in *Of Mice and Men* and the death of a dream, a dream symbolised in the Arthurian legend by the Round Table.

The search for the Holy Grail – an unattainable dream.

One reason for such a link is that it suggests the nobility of the working man, a common theme (see Literary

Links to the old world. Terms) in Steinbeck's work. It is also a feature in some American writing that it sought to link itself to the older traditions of European writing, as if new writers in a new country felt somehow validated by their link with an older tradition as well as refreshed by being able to break from it. There is also an interesting area to

Mythologising American history. examine in the tendency to mythologise (see Literary Terms) aspects of American history, as in the Wild West and in the American Dream. All these point to a possible link with the Arthurian legend, but it is probably best not carried too far. Searching for a better future and betrayal are universal human experiences, and are found in many places and stories as well as in the Arthurian legend.

THE WORKING MAN

It is a little difficult to decide if the working man is merely a subject in the novel, or a theme (see Literary Terms) in its own right. The characters in the book are drawn from a narrow social range, most being working men. Steinbeck reveals the immense diversity of personality and character to be found on a single ranch – the quickwittedness and loyalty of George, the slowness of Lennie, the natural dignity and leadership of Slim, the bitter, ingrowing cynicism of Crooks, the brutality of Carlson, the superficiality of Whit and the sad fatalism of Candy.

Does Steinbeck attempt to arouse your pity by a false, unreal concentration on misfits and cripples? If so, the
Slim – a natural leader. balance is at least partially put right by the portrayal of Slim, by which Steinbeck seems to be saying that natural leaders and people of authority will emerge in every walk of life.

Brains and brawn in American life. There is a tendency in Steinbeck's novels to rate the man with practical skills above the man with intellectual ability. This might appear strange from a

Frontier values. highly intelligent writer, but it is a sub-theme in American culture, again derived from the myth (see Literary Terms) or dream of the frontier. The frontier man had to build his own house, farm his own crops, deliver his own animals of their young, mend and make agricultural machinery, make his own cartridges, skin and cure animal hide and brew his own drink – at least in legend! Yet with all these practical skills (in effect the ability to do at least part of the job of the modern builder, farmer, veterinary surgeon, agricultural engineer, gunsmith, tanner, brewer and carpenter) frontier man often had only one book, a copy of the Holy Bible.

Of Mice and Men does not condemn intellectuals. It merely ignores them and sees real life as taking place outside of their boundaries.

STRUCTURE

Of Mice and Men is a short novel. Sometimes these are described as novellas.

CHAPTER DIVISIONS?

The book has no chapter divisions, but falls into six readily identifiable sections, all except the first and last of which are set in the bunk-house. The division of the novel into six clear sections bears comparison with the separate scenes of a play. There is therefore a dramatic element to the structure of the novel as well as to its style.

The book has a play-like structure.

Why are there no chapter divisions? Probably because in such a short novel Steinbeck does not want to break up the flow of the text. Chapter divisions might also reduce the feeling of inevitability in the novel.

INEVITABILITY

Is Steinbeck clumsy or deliberate?

Steinbeck has been criticised for making the ending seem inevitable, and for dropping too many clumsy hints as to what will happen. The hints are Lennie's killing of mice, the story of what happened between Lennie and the girl in Weed, the killing of Candy's dog, the fight with Curley, the killing of the puppy, the emphasis on Lennie's vast strength, the girl's interest in Lennie and George's oft-repeated assertions that the girl is 'jail-bait' and will bring nothing but trouble. The defence against this charge is that Steinbeck is not writing a novel of suspense, but a novel about characters. It might still be felt that some of the hints he offers are rather heavy handed.

Remember that many types of literature do not require you to be kept in suspense.

STRUCTURE

Chronological order

Of Mice and Men follows a simple chronological, or real time, structure, with no flashbacks to previous episodes and no rushing forward to see snippets of the future, both common techniques in many modern novels. The story commences on a Thursday evening and its climax is reached on the following Sunday afternoon.

The keynote of the plot and structure in this novel is simplicity.

GEORGE

Small
Restless
Intelligent
Practical
Caring
Modest
Tragic

George Milton and Slim are the heroes of *Of Mice and Men*. George is, in Slim's words, 'a smart little guy' (p. 41). It is typical of George that he denies this claim, pointing out that if he was really smart he would be farming for himself and not doing all the work for other people. One of the points made in the novel as a whole is that intelligence on its own is worth little. If it were worth much, then both George and Crooks would be rich men.

Economic reasons make it hard for George to possess his own small farm. There are other difficulties as well, the main one being Lennie. If George is to look after Lennie, probably the only way he can do it is to move from ranch to ranch. The longer the pair stay in one place, the more likely it is that Lennie will get himself into trouble. Permanent employment is not therefore an option, unless George ditches Lennie.

So why does George stay with Lennie? George frequently tells Lennie how much freedom he, George, would enjoy if he was not with Lennie. He says it so often that Lennie knows the speech off by heart, just as he does the speech about the dream of a farm.

Undoubtedly George has come to like Lennie, and he feels a sense of duty and responsibility towards him. But there is more to their partnership than this. George is a thinker. All around him he sees the rootless, nomadic farm workers, many of them lonely, ineffectual and lost. The companionship with Lennie staves off loneliness (see Themes), but it also gives George a role in life, a clear task, looking after Lennie. Early on it made George feel superior. Now it simply makes him different, and even gives him status. In addition, just as there is trouble in being with Lennie, so there is strength, huge strength. Who would fight George if they knew they would have to fight Lennie as well?

George is a good judge of other people's characters. He can sense that Curley and his wife will bring trouble, and that Slim is a good man. He is quiet, causing no trouble in the bunk-house, modest and clearly a good worker. He is clean-living, partly because he needs to save his money if ever he is to buy his farm and cannot waste money in the brothel or in the pool room, but also because of his temperament. He is appalled by Lennie drinking scummy water, appalled by the prospect of the previous occupant of his bunk having left lice in the bedding. He is a peaceful man but fights when he has to. One senses a certain delight when he tells Lennie to 'get' Curley.

Some critics have argued that George shows a great capacity for 'moral growth' over the course of the novel. They argue that his relationship with Lennie matures him, forces him to think more and increases his awareness of moral problems. He certainly has grown up in the past as a result of his relationship with Lennie. Early on he used to show off the power he had over Lennie, forcing him to do stupid and, in one instance, life threatening things. His sense of shame soon stopped him. However, his shooting of Lennie adds nothing new to what we know of him. It is merely the result of everything we have learnt about him and, like so much else in the novel, is almost inevitable. Features which George has possessed all along combine to force him to shoot Lennie.

George is a moral person, as shown by his distaste for brothels and his disgust at Curley telling the story about a glove full of Vaseline. It is George's morality that tells him Lennie cannot be allowed to run away, because this time he has actually killed someone.

George is full of compassion and it is this which makes him wish for a clean death for Lennie, rather than a lynching or a lifetime spent cooped up in jail.

George is a responsible person. He brought Lennie to the farm, and so the responsibility for what happened and the responsibility for the punishment are his. He accepts them, with great heroism. Slim spots that George had to do what he does to Lennie. No one else in the novel is shown as understanding.

George has made sacrifices in order to look after Lennie. When he kills him he makes the greatest sacrifice of all. Lennie dies with the words and expression of their shared dream on his lips and face. When he dies, so does the dream, killed by the man who brought it into being.

The tragedy of George is that his best features have led him to kill the thing and the person he loves most. There is no practical reason why George should not still buy the farm with Candy. Emotionally it is another story. The dream is dead with Lennie and because of Lennie.

LENNIE

Lennie Small is a child's mind in a man's body. The mind is extremely childlike, the body immensely strong. He is a half-wit, a simpleton and his tragedy is that his mind has never learnt how to control his body. He is amazed and upset when his mice and his puppy die, unable to realise that it is not their fragility but his strength that are to blame.

Lennie is also, as is pointed out, a 'nice fella' (p. 36). After his strength his most obvious feature is his innocence, an innocence so transparent and obvious that you cannot help but sympathise with him, and feel some of the same affection that George so obviously

A child's
mind in a
huge man's
body
A 'nice fella'
An innocent
who does not
know his
own strength

feels for him. He is described in terms of an animal often by Steinbeck, perhaps pointing to his being a creature of instinct rather than a being of rational or intellectual thought, but this does nothing to lessen his humanity. Lennie is like an animal in that his mind and his body cannot cope with the complexities of human life. The only way he can cope is to be a like a tame dog, tethered always to his master George and never let out of his master's sight.

Yet Lennie is not totally straightforward. He has an animal cunning that he can bring into play. For instance he realises that George will feel guilty about losing his temper at the start of the novel after he has taken away Lennie's mouse. Lennie plays on George's feelings of guilt that he has robbed a child of a prized possession. As a result of this Lennie gets the sympathy that he wants from George.

Lennie is cunning and aware in another sense. His instinct tells him that the ranch is 'no good place' to be (p. 34), and events prove him correct.

Some critics have felt that Lennie's tendency to hold on when he panics is unrealistic, but anyone who has lifesaved and tried to break the grip of someone they think is drowning will know that hanging on is a trait shared by all human beings, and not just those who are mentally retarded.

A more serious criticism is directed against the two visions Lennie has at the end of the novel, one of Aunt Clara and one of a gigantic rabbit, both of whom reprimand Lennie.

Some would argue that Lennie has been portrayed as someone whose intellect makes it difficult for him to speak at all, never mind give a voice to two other people and construct a dialogue (see Literary Terms). The effect of these two 'visions' could therefore be seen as false and artificial, an artistic intervention in a novel which has above all been realistic.

On the other hand, it could be argued that both Aunt Clara and the rabbit feature largely in Lennie's memory and his mind, and that in one he is remembering what was said to him and in the other merely putting George's words into the mouth of a much-loved animal.

Lennie is both a victim and a symbol (see Literary Terms). It is not his fault that he was born without the full mental faculties of others, and he becomes a victim of a world that chooses not to understand or make allowances for him. He is also a symbol of a world that is rarely just or fair and which exercises a cruel judgement on those who live within it. Only one of those who suffer in *Of Mice and Men* is blameworthy for what he does and deserves his punishment, and that is Curley. The remainder – Candy, Crooks, Curley's wife, George and above all Lennie – suffer despite their basic innocence.

SLIM

Slim receives the longest introductory description of any character in the novel – no less than twenty lines in the edition used in this book. Those who wish to sum up Slim need look no further than that description, which says everything there is to say about Slim. The remainder of the novel simply reinforces the points made in this introduction and adds nothing new.

The length of this introduction shows how deeply interested Steinbeck was in Slim. The description given of him could be used without disrespect of an elder statesman, a great teacher or a philosopher. It might seem ludicrous that it is applied to a ranch hand, albeit a very skilled one.

Honest and
dignified
A man with
natural
authority

It also begs the question as to why someone so gifted is forced to live in a bunk-house, eating another person's food and condemned to live with anyone the boss appoints to work on the ranch.

Slim is the product of Steinbeck's desire to show that nobility of mind and purpose can be found in all sections of society. It is also a part of his mission to raise the status of migrant workers, something he brought to near perfection in his later novel *The Grapes of Wrath* (1939).

It is Slim who understands why George and Lennie work the ranches as a pair, and he understands the bond between them. It is Slim who comes to the only correct judgement of Lennie, that he is both a child and a 'nice fella' (p. 42). It is Slim who is the only person who understands why George has to kill Lennie, and it is Slim who is the only person who comes near to understanding what the personal cost to George has been of doing what he has done. To that extent Slim is the conscience of the novel, the voice of truth and its anchor point.

Does Steinbeck give too much respect to those with practical skills, and ignore those with intellectual ability? Perhaps the answer depends rather too much on which set of skills one was born with. Slim makes a point which few critics of the novel have spotted. Like George, Slim is intelligent, that intelligence being shown in a capacity to sum up situations instantly rather than in any ability to pass examinations. Slim is someone whose self-respect derives from the fact that he does what he is paid to do superbly. In his case it is driving mules or other animals. In another person's case it could be playing superb soccer, writing the best book ever on Shakespeare or cooking the best meals in town. The nature of the skill is not what matters; it is mastery of that skill which counts. Those who know what they can do and are allowed by life to do it well are, in Steinbeck's eyes, the true aristocracy of our world. Slim is just such an aristocrat and in his portrayal Steinbeck is telling us that we should not be surprised to find an aristocrat living in the bunk-house of a Californian ranch. This aristocracy earns its spurs by what it is and what it does, not where it was born or to whom.

Candy

One handed
Pathetic
Subservient
Stooped
Devoted to his dog

Candy has lost his right hand in a farm accident and is now reduced to the meanest job on the ranch, that of 'swamper' or menial cleaner. His function in the novel is to show you what happens to an old man beset by physical disability, loneliness and rejection.

He is a pathetic figure. He has lost all control over his life and can only pass his time through being subservient to others yet getting his own back on them through gossip. Only on two occasions in the novel does he stand up to people, once when he joins in on the attack on Curley, and again when he tells Curley's wife what he thinks of her. In each case his defiance is short lived, and its early demise serves only to make him appear even more pathetic. In that defiance we see both what Candy might have been and what he has become.

Against all this is the fact that you are shown just how little it would take to revitalise Candy – ten acres and a few animals. You are being asked to think how many other outwardly worthless people need so little to make them figures of respect.

Candy provides a parallel to George and Lennie in that he relies on his dog, just as George and Lennie are an elevated version of a master–dog relationship. Candy clings to his dog, despite all that logic and common sense dictate. In much the same manner, George and Lennie cling to each other, perhaps despite the dictates of common sense.

The dog's death reveals that Candy is a human being with all human feelings and emotions and as such should not be lightly dismissed. Candy is old, infirm and weak. One of the strongest statements in *Of Mice and Men* is that such people are worthy of our attention and our respect.

CROOKS

'Stable buck'
Crippled
Pained
Proud

Like Candy, Crooks is an example of Steinbeck's compassion and a further illustration of the way in which loneliness (see Themes) can corrupt and destroy a man. Crooks has a double burden. He is not only a negro in a society that immediately relegates non-whites to a sub-human status, but also a partial cripple in a society that values human being simply on their ability to provide a service.

The true horror of his situation is revealed when he dares to challenge a white woman married to a white man. Curley's wife has done little to warrant respect, though she may have your sympathy. This girl, by virtue of her race rather than her attributes as a human being, can crush Crooks in little more than a sentence. As a white woman even the accusation of rape against a negro will result in the lynching of the negro. It is unjust, unfair and against all concepts of natural justice – yet it is the way of the world.

But if Steinbeck is compassionate, he is also fair. Crooks is not treated badly by the other ranch hands and is described as a 'nice fella' (p. 20) by Candy. He is also given a room of his own, albeit a room in which he also works and which is, as Candy points out, by a manure heap.

Crooks's structural role in the novel is to appear two thirds of the way through and forewarn and prepare you for the imminent destruction of George and Lennie's dream. In creating a character (see Literary Terms) such as Crooks, Steinbeck is following a time-hallowed tradition.

First, find a character in whom you have to believe, because he or she is so convincingly drawn and you identify with them. Then expose him or her to a potent dream and show him or her warming to it as you have warmed to it. Finally, show the character realising that the dream is nothing more than a dream, a fantasy doomed to failure because the real world does not allow dreams to come to fruition.

Like Crooks we want to believe in the dream despite everything we know. And like Crooks we come to realise that it is an impossible dream.

CURLEY

Small
Quick
Unpleasant
Jealous
Unfaithful

Curley is a spoilt, restless young man with a grudge against the world. A small man, he is incapable of meeting someone bigger without taking a dislike to them, and he seems set on proving to the world that he is a big man in all but size. He has had some success as an amateur boxer and boxing has become an obsession with him, so much so that every person he meets is seen as a possible opponent.

Curley makes obscene allusions to his young wife and goes to the brothel on Saturday nights. He then complains when his wife appears to want to take her pleasure in a similar vein. He is a laughing stock with the other men for his obsession that she is behaving herself, and is hated by his new wife.

Curley is not unintelligent, and has a form of cunning. He is also cruel and insensitive, capable only of seeing

Picks fights to prove his toughness

the world through his own eyes and as a result possessed of a supreme selfishness. He is a man bordering on evil, and is by far the most unpleasant and unattractive character in the novel. His inability to control his wife or even vaguely to understand her brings about the final tragedy of Lennie's death. He is to blame, just as much as his wife and as Lennie. His tragedy is that he will never accept that blame. For Curley, it is always someone else's fault.

CURLEY'S WIFE

Curley's wife is a 'tart' (p. 30) and may well be 'jail bait' (p. 34) in the eyes of the ranch hands, but she is never really evil. Her punishment outweighs any crimes she may have committed. Perhaps she could even have been a loving wife had she met the right man. Steinbeck certainly felt that she would have been a slave to any man who 'treated her like a person'.

'Jail bait'
Flirtatious
A dreamer
Lonely
Misunderstood

We know more about Steinbeck's feelings towards Curley's wife than about any other character. In the famous 'Miss Luce' letter, he wrote to the actress playing the part in the stage version of the novel, saying how he saw the character (see Literary Terms). Steinbeck says she is essentially a good and trusting person who grew up 'in an atmosphere of fighting and suspicion'. Her pretence of hardness is largely a sham. It is all she knows. She is not particularly over-sexed, but has been forced to recognise that her sexuality is the only weapon she has, and the only thing that gets her noticed. She was almost certainly a virgin before she married Curley because she has had it preached at her so hard that it is the only way she can get a husband. In Steinbeck's words, 'She had only that one thing to sell and she knew it'. A comparison has been made here (though not by Steinbeck) with another semi-mythical figure in American entertainment, the film actress Marilyn Monroe, capable of exuding a huge sexuality but combining it with innocence, vulnerability and an inability to enjoy sex.

There is, of course, a danger in knowing so much about what the author intended the character to be like. If every author's intention was what actually got written then every novel would be a bestseller. An author can tell us how he intended the character to be; the reader is the one who decides what is actually described. Is there a case for seeing Curley's wife as rather more of a hard case than Steinbeck intended her to be?

MINOR CHARACTERS

THE BOSS
A stocky, short little man. He is a reasonable sort of person, who gets angry at times but buys whisky for the hands at Christmas. He is a very distant figure. His wife is never mentioned and it might be assumed that she is dead.

CARLSON
A powerful, insensitive and large stomached ranch hand. He objects to the smell of Candy's dog, pressurises Candy to have it shot and does the business himself with evident satisfaction, using his own Luger pistol. This is the same pistol that George later uses to shoot Lennie.

WHIT
A young ranch hand, who finds a letter in a magazine written by an ex-worker at the ranch. He is very superficial, and has no real involvement in the plot of the novel or its themes (see Literary Terms), except as the hand who is sent into the town to fetch the deputy sheriff after the murder of Curley's wife.

There are almost two separate styles in *Of Mice and Men*. One is descriptive and almost poetic in its intensity, the other down-to-earth and colloquial. It is a major achievement of Steinbeck to blend these two styles together with almost complete fluency.

Descriptive style

This owes its success to Steinbeck's eye for minute observation of nature and his gift for unusual metaphors and similes (see Literary Terms). As one example, he describes the head of a water-snake as being 'like a periscope' (p. 8). At first reading this simile might seem totally out of place. A periscope is a man-made object of steel and glass, part of a machine designed for war and found at sea rather than in the confines of a small pool in a river. Yet the image (see Literary Terms) does work. It is startling and unexpected, and so focuses your attention on what is being described. Visually the two are similar, with both being upright and ploughing through the water. The snake's eyes are in its head, just as the periscope provides eyes for the submarine. A submarine is a machine of death, but so perhaps is the snake, hunting for its kill in the shadows.

Steinbeck's use of light.

Steinbeck loves to use light in his descriptive passages. The light flaming on the Gabilan Mountains is a recurrent image. Steinbeck is fascinated by sunlight. He describes a bar of it shining into the bunk-house. Later Curley's wife enters the bunk-house and cuts out the light – the light being used as a symbol (see Literary Terms).

Sound and vision.

Steinbeck also uses sound in his descriptions, particularly the background sounds that add so much to our imagination of the colour and vision of a scene. One example is the distant clang of horseshoes in the yard; another the far off shouts on the highway as the pursuers close in on Lennie. The accuracy of this observation helps you to believe that you are an eye witness to the events described.

Colloquial   Steinbeck makes heavy use of dialogue (see Literary
language   Terms), and recreates directly the vernacular, slangy and
colloquial language of the ranch hands. He writes as
they speak, and recreates their language with
unfaltering accuracy. In doing so he uses swear words
and contortions of grammar that would have an
English teacher in hospital (my favourite is 'Ain't got no
relatives nor nothing' (p. 63), which in grammar terms
is actually a treble negative, something almost
impossible to achieve). The language may be
grammatically incorrect. Yet it is vivid, alive and full of
colour. Steinbeck also uses it for comic effect. Slim is
described as the aristocrat of the ranch, its true king.
After this introduction, his first words are, 'It's
brighter'n a bitch outside' (p. 36), a line which no king
would use and which brings you back down to earth
very rapidly.

There is irony (see Literary Terms) in much of
Steinbeck's dialogue. Candy suggests Crooks's room is
cosy and that he is lucky to have a room on his own.
Crooks replies that it's 'swell' (p. 79), particularly with a
manure pile under the window.

These two aspects of Steinbeck's writing – his use of
colloquial language and his descriptive style – have been
described as 'jewelled metaphors' and the 'practical
language of fact'. The blending of the two is one of the
reasons why *Of Mice and Men is* such a remarkable
novel.

PART FOUR

STUDY SKILLS

HOW TO USE QUOTATIONS

One of the secrets of success in writing essays is the way you use quotations. There are five basic principles:

- Put inverted commas at the beginning and end of the quotation
- Write the quotation exactly as it appears in the orginal
- Do not use a quotation that repeats what you have just written
- Use the quotation so that it fits into your sentence
- Keep the quotation as short as possible

Quotations should be used to develop the line of thought in your essays. Your comment should not duplicate what is in your quotation. For example:

Those who work on the ranch seem to think that the Boss is a reasonable employer. George asks what he is like, and Candy's response is this, '"He's a nice fella," the swamper agreed. "You got to take him right"'.

Far more effective is to write:

Those who work on the ranch seem to agree with Candy that the boss is 'a nice fella'.

However, the most sophisticated way of using the writer's words is to embed them into your sentence:

You know that George has done the right thing when Slim says, 'You hadda, George. I swear you hadda'.

When you use quotations in this way, you are demonstating the ability to use text as evidence to support your ideas – not simply including words form the original to prove you have read it.

Everyone writes differently. Work through the suggestions given here and adapt the advice to suit your own style and interests. This will improve your essay writing skills and allow your personal voice to emerge.

The following points indicate in ascending order the skills of essay writing:

- Picking out one or two facts about the story and adding the odd detail
- Writing about the text by retelling the story
- Retelling the story and adding a quotation here and there
- Organising an answer which explains what is happening in the text and giving quotations to support what you write

- Writing in such a way as to show that you have thought about the intentions of the writer of the text and that you understand the techniques used
- Writing at some length, giving you viewpoint on the text and commenting by picking out details to support your views
- Looking at the text as a work of art, demonstrating clear critical judgement and explaining to the reader of your essay how the enjoyment of the text is assisted by literary devices, linguistic effects and psychological insights; showing how the text relates to the time when it was written

The dotted line above represents the division between lower and higher level grades. Higher-level performance begins when you start to consider your response as a reader of the text. The highest level is reached when you offer an enthusiastic personal response and show how this piece of literature is a product of its time.

Coursework
essay

Set aside an hour or so at the start of your work to plan what you have to do.

- List all the points you feel are needed to cover the task. Collect page references of information and quotations that will support what you have to say. A helpful tool is the highlighter pen: this saves painstaking copying and enables you to target precisely what you want to use.
- Focus on what you consider to be the main points of the essay. Try to sum up your argument in a single sentence, which could be the closing sentence of your essay. Depending on the essay title, it could be a statement about a character: Slim is the real hero of the novel because he is the only character who reaches the right conclusions about everything'; an opinion about setting: The authority with which Steinbeck describes the countryside around Salinas and the life of the ranch hand – both of which he had personally experienced – gives authority to everything else he states in the novel'; or a judgement on a theme: I think loneliness is the major theme in *Of Mice and Men* because more people suffer from it in the novel than from anything else.
- Make a short essay plan. Use the first paragraph to introduce the argument you wish to make. In the following paragraphs develop this argument with details, examples and other possible points of view. Sum up your argument in the last paragraph. Check you have answered the question.
- Write the essay, remembering all the time the central point your are making.
- On completion, go back over what you have written to eliminate careless errors and improve expression. Read it aloud to yourself, or, if you are feeling more confident, to a relative or friend.

If you can, try to type your essay, using a word processor. This will allow you to correct and improve your writing without spoiling its appearance.

Examination essay

The essay written in an examination often carries more marks than the coursework essay even though it is written under considerable time pressure.

In the revision period build up notes on various aspects of the text you are using. Fortunately, in acquiring this set of York Notes on *Of Mice and Men*, you have made a prudent beginning! York Notes are set out to give you vital information and help you to construct your personal overview of the text.

Make notes with appropriate quotations about the key issues of the set text. Go into the examination knowing your text and having a clear set of opinions about it.

In the examination

In most English Literature examinations, you can take in copies of your set books. This is an enormous advantage although it may lull you into a false sense of security. Beware! There is simply not enough time in an examination to read the book from scratch.

- Read the question paper carefully and remind yourself what you have to do.
- Look at the questions on your set texts to select the one that most interests you and mentally work out the points you wish to stress.
- Remind yourself of the time available and how you are going to use it.
- Briefly map out a short plan in note form that will keep your writing on track and illustrate the key argument you want to make.
- Then set about writing it.
- When you have finished, check through to eliminate errors.

To summarise,   • **Know the text**
these are the   • **Have a clear understanding of and opinions on the storyline,**
keys to success: **characters, setting, themes and writer's concerns**
                   • **Select the right material**
                   • **Plan and write a clear response, continually bearing the question in mind**

SAMPLE ESSAY PLAN

A typical essay question on *Of Mice and Men* is followed by a sample essay plan in note form. This does not present the only answer to the question, merely one answer. Do not be afraid to include your own ideas, and leave out some of those in the sample! Remember that quotations are essential to prove and illustrate the points you make.

To what extent is *Of Mice and Men* a novel of protest?

Introduction   Steinbeck's most famous novel, *The Grapes of Wrath*, is a protest novel. But it is wrong to judge one novel on basis of another.

Part 1   There is certainly much protest in the novel

• against treatment of old people (Candy and dog)
• against racism (Crooks)
• against those who work land not reaping its rewards
• protest against loneliness (Candy, Crooks, George and Lennie)

Part 2   There are some areas, however, where there is no protest at all

• against treatment of people with special needs (Lennie)
• no complaint against ranch owner ('nice fella')
• ranch hands seem to live quite well

y

- no protest against what George does to Lennie, just sad acceptance ('You hadda, George')

Part 3   The label 'novel of protest' does not do justice to the book in terms of its

- compassion and care for individuals
- grasp of the beauties of nature
- treatment of people's need to dream
- vision of freedom
- treatment of the theme of loneliness

Conclusion   *Of Mice and Men* is a novel of compassion. It does not protest about life. It observes life and recreates it, leaving you to judge.

FURTHER QUESTIONS

1 Are there any weaknesses in *Of Mice and Men*?
2 To what extent is Steinbeck's style 'dramatic' in *Of Mice and Men*?
3 What contribution does Slim make to *Of Mice and Men*?
4 Is *Of Mice and Men* a pessimistic novel?
5 Does Steinbeck condemn Curley's wife, or does he sympathise with her?
6 Why does George shoot Lennie?
7 What are the main techniques that Steinbeck uses to create atmosphere in *Of Mice and Men*?
8 How significant is the theme of loneliness in *Of Mice and Men*?
9 'There are too many cripples, misfits and unusual characters in *Of Mice and Men* for it to be described accurately as true to life.' Discuss.
10 What is the importance of dreams and dreaming to the success of *Of Mice and Men*?

PART FIVE

CULTURAL CONNECTIONS

BROADER PERSPECTIVES

Anyone studying *Of Mice and Men* should also read
what is usually thought of as Steinbeck's greatest work,
The Grapes of Wrath (1939). It is different from *Of Mice
and Men*, but noting the differences reveals the
strengths (and perhaps the weaknesses) of the two
books. Of his other novels, *Tortilla Flat* (1935) and
Cannery Row (1944) are both short and very readable.

Of Mice and Men has been filmed three times, and most
critics agree that the earliest version, directed by Lewis
Milestone (1939), is the most impressive. This film was
ahead of its time in having the action start before the
credits (almost unheard of at the time), and has a gritty
realism that may have been influenced by the then-
recent Depression. The performance of Lon Chaney as
Lennie is often seen as the standard all others have to
aim for. Its music is by Aaron Copland and is highly
regarded.

A 1981 version for television was made as the result of
a lifelong ambition on the part of producer/star Robert
Blake. It is hard to get hold of, but is seen as an above
average production.

The most modern version was directed by Gary Sinese
in 1992. The photography is excellent, but some
criticisms (not universal) have been raised as to the
acting of George, Lennie and Curley's wife.

Do see these films (and John Ford's excellent 1940
version of *The Grapes of Wrath*) - *but only after you have
read the novel*. Ask yourself if the director's vision of the
novel matches the vision you had in your head after you
had read it. Does the film merely seek to repeat in
visual form what Steinbeck did in print? Or do the
films go beyond what Steinbeck wrote?

Many films have emulated the pairing of George and Lennie. Watch *Rain Man* (1988), for instance, and look at the relationship between Raymond and Charlie. Or, for a different perspective on Lennie, see the James Whale *Frankenstein*, made in 1931. The monster finds a small girl throwing flowers into a lake. Thinking that she will float like the flowers, the monster accidentally drowns her. A lynch mob is raised that chases him to his death.

There are a number of good biographies of Steinbeck. The student who wishes to be adventurous should read *Conversations with John Steinbeck*, edited by Thomas Fensch (1988). This is a fascinating insight into the mind of a great writer and says a great deal about how and why he wrote as he did.

characterisation the techniques by which an author describes and tries to bring to life the characters in his or her work. There are as many variations in this as there are characters, and characterisation that is both convincing and realistic is essential to the success of any novel.

dialogue the speech and conversation of characters in a novel, play or poem. Capturing the 'feel' of real speech is one of the hardest things a novelist has to do.

image, imagery a word-picture that describes some scene, person or object. More often the term is used of similes or metaphors (see below). Authors often draw their images from certain areas. Steinbeck favours natural imagery, and images based on light.

irony saying one thing while meaning another. Crooks is being ironic when he says it is 'swell' to have a room with a manure heap outside the window.

metaphor a description in which a person or object is described as being something else, as in the water-snake, 'twisting its periscope head'.

motif a theme, character or image that recurs again and again in a novel or work of literature. The rabbits in Lennie's dreams and mind are a motif, running like a theme tune through the novel.

myth/mythologising myth has two meanings. The common one of something that is untrue ('It is a myth that ...') should not be confused with its literary meaning. A myth is a story often associated with religious beliefs, based on supernatural or god-like characters, and commenting on issues central to human existence. The central story of a myth can be adapted and rewritten to fit other times, and such famous works as Shelley's *Prometheus Unbound* (1820) or J.R.R. Tolkien's *The Lord of the Rings* (1954–55) rework one or more established myths. An author can, of course, attempt to create a myth as well as to use an existing one.

paradox usually an apparent contradiction that on closer examination turns out not to be a contradiction at all. It usually relies on placing two opposites alongside each other. One paradox in the novel is George's decision to kill Lennie in order to protect him, based on the paradox of being cruel to be kind. There is also a form of paradox in the dream that can never be realised, shared by George and Lennie.

simile a description in which a person or object is described as being as or like something else, as in, 'in rolled clusters, like sausages'.

symbol an image that describes far more than the physical features of the object described. The heron that kills the water-snake is a physical object but it is also a symbol of nature, telling you what it stands for and what it contains.

theme central idea or ideas that are examined with a view to some serious uestions being asked, and some conclusions being drawn; the overriding topic or topics that interest a writer in his book. Loneliness is a theme in *Of Mice and Men*.

TEST ANSWERS

TEST YOURSELF (Pages 1–18)

A
••• 1 George
2 Lennie
3 Lennie
4 George
5 George
6 Bus driver
7 Aunt Clara

TEST YOURSELF (Pages 18–39)

A
••• 1 Curley
2 Candy
3 Carlson
4 Slim
5 Lennie
6 The boss
7 Curly
8 Slim

TEST YOURSELF (Pages 40–69)

A
••• 1 George
2 Carlson
3 George
4 Candy
5 Curley
6 Lennie
7 Lennie
8 Crooks
9 Lennie

TEST YOURSELF (Pages 69–113)

A
••• 1 Crooks
2 Candy
3 Curley's wife
4 Crooks
5 Lennie
6 Crooks
7 Curley
8 Curley's wife
9 George and Slim

NOTES

NOTES

NOTES

NOTES

NOTES

NOTES

NOTES

GCSE and equivalent levels (£3.50 each)

Harold Brighouse
Hobson's Choice

Charles Dickens
Great Expectations

Charles Dickens
Hard Times

George Eliot
Silas Marner

William Golding
Lord of the Flies

Thomas Hardy
The Mayor of Casterbridge

Susan Hill
I'm the King of the Castle

Barry Hines
A Kestrel for a Knave

Harper Lee
To Kill a Mockingbird

Arthur Miller
A View from the Bridge

Arthur Miller
The Crucible

George Orwell
Animal Farm

J.B. Priestley
An Inspector Calls

J.D. Salinger
The Catcher in the Rye

William Shakespeare
Macbeth

William Shakespeare
The Merchant of Venice

William Shakespeare
Romeo and Juliet

William Shakespeare
Twelfth Night

George Bernard Shaw
Pygmalion

John Steinbeck
Of Mice and Men

Mildred D. Taylor
Roll of Thunder, Hear My Cry

James Watson
Talking in Whispers

A Choice of Poets

Nineteenth Century Short Stories

Poetry of the First World War

FORTHCOMING TITLES IN THE SERIES

Advanced level (£3.99 each)

Margaret Atwood
The Handmaid's Tale

Jane Austen
Emma

Jane Austen
Pride and Prejudice

William Blake
Poems/Songs of Innocence and Songs of Experience

Charlotte Brontë
Jane Eyre

Emily Brontë
Wuthering Heights

Geoffrey Chaucer
Wife of Bath's Prologue and Tale

Joseph Conrad
Heart of Darkness

Charles Dickens
Great Expectations

F. Scott Fitzgerald
The Great Gatsby

Thomas Hardy
Tess of the D'Urbervilles

Seamus Heaney
Selected Poems

James Joyce
Dubliners

Arthur Miller
Death of a Salesman

William Shakespeare
Antony and Cleopatra

William Shakespeare
Hamlet

William Shakespeare
King Lear

William Shakespeare
The Merchant of Venice

William Shakespeare
Much Ado About Nothing

William Shakespeare
Othello

William Shakespeare
Romeo and Juliet

William Shakespeare
The Tempest

Mary Shelley
Frankenstein

Alice Walker
The Color Purple

John Webster
The Duchess of Malfi

Tennessee Williams
A Streetcar Named Desire

Chinua Achebe
Things Fall Apart

Edward Albee
Who's Afraid of Virginia Woolf?

Jane Austen
Mansfield Park

Jane Austen
Northanger Abbey

Jane Austen
Persuasion

Jane Austen
Sense and Sensibility

Samuel Beckett
Waiting for Godot

Alan Bennett
Talking Heads

John Betjeman
Selected Poems

Robert Bolt
A Man for All Seasons

Charlotte Brontë
Jane Eyre

Robert Burns
Selected Poems

Lord Byron
Selected Poems

Geoffrey Chaucer
The Franklin's Tale

Geoffrey Chaucer
The Merchant's Tale

Geoffrey Chaucer
The Nun's Priest's Tale

Geoffrey Chaucer
Prologue to the Canterbury Tales

Samuel Taylor Coleridge
Selected Poems

Daniel Defoe
Moll Flanders

Daniel Defoe
Robinson Crusoe

Shelagh Delaney
A Taste of Honey

Charles Dickens
Bleak House

Charles Dickens
David Copperfield

Charles Dickens
Oliver Twist

Emily Dickinson
Selected Poems

John Donne
Selected Poems

Douglas Dunn
Selected Poems

George Eliot
Middlemarch

George Eliot
The Mill on the Floss

T.S. Eliot
The Waste Land

T.S. Eliot
Selected Poems

Henry Fielding
Joseph Andrews

E.M. Forster
Howards End

E.M. Forster
A Passage to India

John Fowles
The French Lieutenant's Woman

Brian Friel
Translations

Elizabeth Gaskell
North and South

Oliver Goldsmith
She Stoops to Conquer

Graham Greene
Brighton Rock

Thomas Hardy
Far from the Madding Crowd

Thomas Hardy
Jude the Obscure

Thomas Hardy
Selected Poems

L.P. Hartley
The Go-Between

Nathaniel Hawthorne
The Scarlet Letter

Ernest Hemingway
The Old Man and the Sea

Homer
The Iliad

Homer
The Odyssey

Aldous Huxley
Brave New World

Ben Jonson
The Alchemist

Ben Jonson
Volpone

James Joyce
A Portrait of the Artist as a Young Man

John Keats
Selected Poems

Philip Larkin
Selected Poems

D.H. Lawrence
The Rainbow

D.H. Lawrence
Sons and Lovers

D.H. Lawrence
Women in Love

Laurie Lee
Cider with Rosie

Christopher Marlowe
Doctor Faustus

Arthur Miller
Death of a Salesman

John Milton
Paradise Lost Bks I & II

John Milton
Paradise Lost IV & IX

Sean O'Casey
Juno and the Paycock

George Orwell
Nineteen Eighty-four

John Osborne
Look Back in Anger

Wilfred Owen
Selected Poems

Harold Pinter
The Caretaker

Sylvia Plath
Selected Works

Alexander Pope
Selected Poems

Jean Rhys
Wide Sargasso Sea

William Shakespeare
As You Like It

William Shakespeare
Coriolanus

William Shakespeare
Henry IV Pt 1

William Shakespeare
Henry V

William Shakespeare
Julius Caesar

William Shakespeare
Measure for Measure

William Shakespeare
Much Ado About Nothing

William Shakespeare
A Midsummer Night's Dream

William Shakespeare
Richard II

William Shakespeare
Richard III

William Shakespeare
Sonnets

William Shakespeare
The Taming of the Shrew

William Shakespeare
The Tempest

William Shakespeare
The Winter's Tale

George Bernard Shaw
Arms and the Man

George Bernard Shaw
Saint Joan

Richard Brinsley Sheridan
The Rivals

R.C. Sherriff
Journey's End

Muriel Spark
The Prime of Miss Jean Brodie

John Steinbeck
The Grapes of Wrath

John Steinbeck
The Pearl

Tom Stoppard
Rosencrantz and Guildenstern are Dead

Jonathan Swift
Gulliver's Travels

John Millington Synge
The Playboy of the Western World

W.M. Thackeray
Vanity Fair

Mark Twain
Huckleberry Finn

Virgil
The Aeneid

Derek Walcott
Selected Poems

Oscar Wilde
The Importance of Being Earnest

Tennessee Williams
Cat on a Hot Tin Roof

Tennessee Williams
The Glass Menagerie

Tennessee Williams
A Streetcar Named Desire

Virginia Woolf
Mrs Dalloway

Virginia Woolf
To the Lighthouse

William Wordsworth
Selected Poems

W.B. Yeats
Selected Poems

York Notes – the Ultimate Literature Guides

York Notes are recognised as the best literature study guides.
If you have enjoyed using this book and have found it useful, you
can now order others directly from us – simply follow the ordering
instructions below.

HOW TO ORDER

Decide which title(s) you require and then order in one of the following
ways:

Booksellers
All titles available from good bookstores.

By post
List the title(s) you require in the space provided overleaf,
select your method of payment, complete your name and
address details and return your completed order form and
payment to:

> *Addison Wesley Longman Ltd*
> *PO BOX 88*
> *Harlow*
> *Essex CM19 5SR*

By phone
Call our Customer Information Centre on 01279 623923 to
place your order, quoting mail number: HEYN1.

By fax
Complete the order form overleaf, ensuring you fill in your
name and address details and method of payment, and fax it
to us on 01279 414130.

By e-mail
E-mail your order to us on awlhe.orders@awl.co.uk listing
title(s) and quantity required and providing full name and
address details as requested overleaf. Please
quote mail number: HEYN1. Please do not
send credit card details by e-mail.

York Notes Order Form

Titles required:

Quantity	Title/ISBN	Price

Sub total _____

Please add £2.50 postage & packing _____

(P & P is free for orders over £50) _____

Total _____

Mail no: HEYN1

Your Name _____

Your Address _____

Postcode _____   Telephone _____

Method of payment

☐ I enclose a cheque or a P/O for £_____ made payable to
Addison Wesley Longman Ltd

☐ Please charge my Visa/Access/AMEX/Diners Club card
Number _____   Expiry Date _____
Signature _____   Date _____

(please ensure that the address given above is the same as for your credit card)

Prices and other details are correct at time of going to press but may change without notice. All orders are subject to status.

☐ *Please tick this box if you would like a complete listing of Longman Study Guides (suitable for GCSE and A-level students)*

York Press

Longman

Addison
Wesley
Longman